Group's
HeartSpa™
Where Women Are Refreshed in Jesus

HEARTSPA ENHANCEMENTS

TOTE BAG
You have a lot to carry—journals, linens, and Bibles. This attractive tote bag makes it easy, and will last for years to come.

UPC 646847-10928-7 $5.99 each

STICKERS
A great way to remember the experience of HeartSpa—use them on invitations, scrapbooks, and more!

ISBN 978-0-7644-2999-6 $3.99/set of 5 sheets

CHARM
These delicate pewter charms can be added to a bracelet or necklace as a keepsake of the memories shared at HeartSpa.

UPC 646847-10931-7 $6.99 each

actual size

MEMORY GIFT BAG
The soothing scents of HeartSpa are captured in this aromatic lavender-scented lotion and handmade complexion soap, all gathered together in a sparkly shimmer bag.

UPC 646847-10963-8 $4.99 each

Order today at www.group.com/heartspa

Group's

Heart Spa™

Where Women Are Refreshed in Jesus

Journal

THIS JOURNAL PRESENTED TO

_____

ON

_____

"O LORD, YOU HAVE EXAMINED MY HEART
AND KNOW EVERYTHING ABOUT ME" (PSALM 139:1).

Group
Loveland, Colorado

Group's HeartSpa™
Where Women Are Refreshed in Jesus

HeartSpa™ Journal
Copyright © 2006 Group Publishing, Inc.

Visit our Web site: **www.group.com**

Credits
Contributing Authors: Linda Crawford and Barbara Gobbs
Creative Development Editor: Amy Nappa
Chief Creative Officer: Joani Schultz
Copy Editor: Jessica Broderick
Art Director/Illustrator: Andrea Filer
Print Production Artist: Veronica Lucas
Cover Photographer: Rodney Stewart
Production Manager: Peggy Naylor

ISBN 0-7644-2945-0
ISBN 978-0-7644-2945-3
Printed in the United States of America.
10 9 8 7 6 5 4 3 2 1   15 14 13 12 11 10 09 08 07 06

Welcome to HeartSpa™!

Are you ready for a getaway experience filled with fun and friends as well as refreshment and relaxation? You'll find all this and more at HeartSpa!

You'll use this journal throughout your HeartSpa Getaway, so keep it handy. It includes Scripture readings, discussion questions, and instructions for some of your activities. Plus, we've added devotions and journaling questions for you to use when you return home, so you can keep your heart refreshed long after HeartSpa is over.

Here's what's inside:

Read:

Let's agree now that what we share in our
HeartSpa Group will stay here. We want to be
able to share with one another without feeling
like others are going to gossip about us. Agreed?
Then let's get started!

- How do you feel about putting something out where others can take it?

- What are other situations where you feel vulnerable?

- What good things can come from being vulnerable with others?

⁴[Jesus] had to go through Samaria on the way. ⁵Eventually he came to the Samaritan village of Sychar, near the field that Jacob gave to his son Joseph. ⁶Jacob's well was there; and Jesus, tired from the long walk, sat wearily beside the well about noontime. ⁷Soon a Samaritan woman came to draw water, and Jesus said to her, "Please give me a drink." ⁸He was alone at the time because his disciples had gone into the village to buy some food.

Bible Insight

Most women gathered at the well in the cool of the early morning and again in the evening—both to accomplish their task and to visit. Since this woman came at the hottest part of the day to draw water, it's likely she was trying to avoid the other women.

⁹The woman was surprised, for Jews refuse to have anything to do with Samaritans. She said to Jesus, "You are a Jew, and I am a Samaritan woman. Why are you asking me for a drink?"

¹⁰Jesus replied, "If you only knew the gift God has for you and who you are speaking to, you would ask me, and I would give you living water."

¹¹"But sir, you don't have a rope or a bucket," she said, "and this well is very deep. Where would you get this living water? ¹²And besides, do you think you're greater than our ancestor Jacob, who gave us this well? How can you offer better water than he and his sons and his animals enjoyed?"

¹³Jesus replied, "Anyone who drinks this water will soon become thirsty again. ¹⁴But those who drink the water I give will never be thirsty again. It becomes a fresh, bubbling spring within them, giving them eternal life."

¹⁵"Please sir," the woman said, "give me this water! Then I'll never be thirsty again, and I won't have to come here to get water."

¹⁶"Go and get your husband," Jesus told her.

¹⁷"I don't have a husband," the woman replied.

Jesus said, "You're right! You don't have a husband—¹⁸for you have had five husbands, and you aren't even married to the man you're living with now. You certainly spoke the truth!"

¹⁹"Sir," the woman said, "you must be a prophet. ²⁰So tell me, why is it that you Jews insist that Jerusalem is the only place of worship, while we Samaritans claim it is here at Mount Gerizim, where our ancestors worshiped?"

²¹Jesus replied, "Believe me, dear woman, the time is coming when it will no longer matter whether you worship the Father on this mountain or in Jerusalem. ²²You Samaritans know very little about the one you worship, while we Jews know all about him, for salvation comes through the Jews. ²³But the time is coming—indeed it's here now—when true worshipers will worship the Father in spirit and in truth.

Bible Insight

Samaritans were Jews who had married with foreigners, making an "impure" race. The Jews despised them and avoided any contact with Samaritans. The Samaritans set up an alternate place to worship on Mount Gerizim, but by the time of this account, that site had been destroyed.

Woman at the Well

The Father is looking for those who will worship him that way. [24]For God is Spirit, so those who worship him must worship in spirit and in truth."

[25]The woman said, "I know the Messiah is coming—the one who is called Christ. When he comes, he will explain everything to us."

[26]Then Jesus told her, "I AM the Messiah!"

[27]Just then his disciples came back. They were shocked to find him talking to a woman, but none of them had the nerve to ask, "What do you want with her?" or "Why are you talking to her?" [28]The woman left her water jar beside the well and ran back to the village, telling everyone,

[29]"Come and see a man who told me everything I ever did! Could he possibly be the Messiah?" [30]So the people came streaming from the village to see him...

[39]Many Samaritans from the village believed in Jesus because the woman had said, "He told me everything I ever did!" [40]When they came out to see him, they begged him to stay in their village. So he stayed for two days,[41]long enough for many more to hear his message and believe. [42]Then they said to the woman, "Now we believe, not just because of what you told us, but because we have heard him ourselves. Now we know that he is indeed the Savior of the world."

Read:

The woman in this account was vulnerable. She'd experienced the cruel and catty comments of others, and she avoided being at the well when other women gathered there to visit. She was trying to protect herself in a vulnerable situation.

Share:

Tell about a time you felt vulnerable and wanted to avoid others.

Read:

The woman at the well could hide from others, but she couldn't hide from Jesus. He knew her.

Sometimes we, like the woman at the well, experience deeper growth or refreshment in our faith when we're in vulnerable situations. These are the times we're aware of Jesus reaching out to us with his love.

Consider the vulnerable situation you just shared with your HeartSpa Group. How can you see Jesus using this situation to draw you to him?

Got Water?

- *What words describe this sponge?*

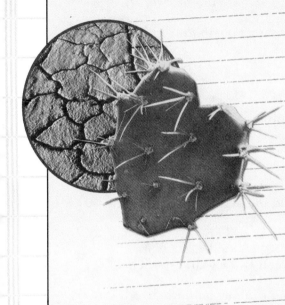

- What changes do you notice in the sponge?

How does Jesus cleanse?

How does Jesus nourish?

How does Jesus dissolve?

Read the following passage aloud. Then, together, discuss your answers to the questions on page 15.

PSALM 42:1-2

"As the deer longs for streams of water, so I long for you, O God. I thirst for God, the living God. When can I go and stand before him?"

BIBLE BACKGROUND

The psalmist not only longed for God, but also longed to be in his presence. A virtuous person would feel comfortable coming before God, while an immoral person would desire nothing more than to run away.

• The author of this psalm uses the image of a thirsty deer to express his longing for God. What is a different image that is more relevant to your life?

🖉 _____
_____
_____
_____
_____

• What are other words for "thirst"? Reread this passage using the new words.

🖉 _____
_____
_____
_____
_____

• When have you felt thirsty for God?

🖉 _____
_____
_____
_____
_____

Lavender

GROUP

*Read the following passages aloud.
Then, together, discuss your answers
to the questions on page 17.*

ISAIAH 55:1

"Is anyone thirsty? Come and drink—even if you have

no money! Come, take your choice of wine or

milk—it's all free!"

REVELATION 22:17

"The Spirit and the bride say, 'Come.' Let anyone

who hears this say, 'Come.' Let anyone who is thirsty

come. Let anyone who desires drink freely from the

water of life."

BIBLE BACKGROUND

The "bride" mentioned in this passage refers to the

church. This invitation is offered by Jesus and by his

followers to join in the delight of being a part of

God's family.

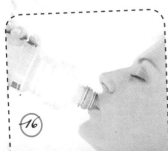

- What are the implications of these verses?

  🖉 _____
  _____
  _____
  _____
  _____
  _____
  _____

- Why is it significant that no money is needed?

  🖉 _____
  _____
  _____
  _____

- What does it mean to drink freely from the water of life?

  🖉 _____
  _____
  _____
  _____
  _____

Read the following passage aloud.
Then, together, discuss your answers
to the questions on page 19.

JEREMIAH 2:13

"For my people have done two evil things:
They have abandoned me—the fountain of
living water. And they have dug for themselves
cracked cisterns that can hold no water at all!"

BIBLE BACKGROUND

In the book of Jeremiah, God pleads with his
people to return to him. God longs to extend
grace to those who will turn to him and accept it.

• What are the key ideas in this verse?

🖉 _____
_____
_____
_____
_____
_____
_____
_____
_____

• What is an example of digging a cracked cistern that women today could relate to?

🖉 _____
_____
_____
_____
_____
_____
_____
_____
_____

My Heart Spa Group

Name: _____

Address: _____

Phone number: _____

E-mail: _____

Name: _____

Address: _____

Phone number: _____

E-mail: _____

Name: _____

Address: _____

Phone number: _____

E-mail: _____

Our Get-Together Plan

Sure, you can get together for coffee or lunch. But what about secretly cleaning the home of someone in need? Or getting together to make a meal? How about putting your newfound spa expertise into action and pampering a woman who didn't get to come on the HeartSpa Getaway? Be creative! Have fun!

Refresh

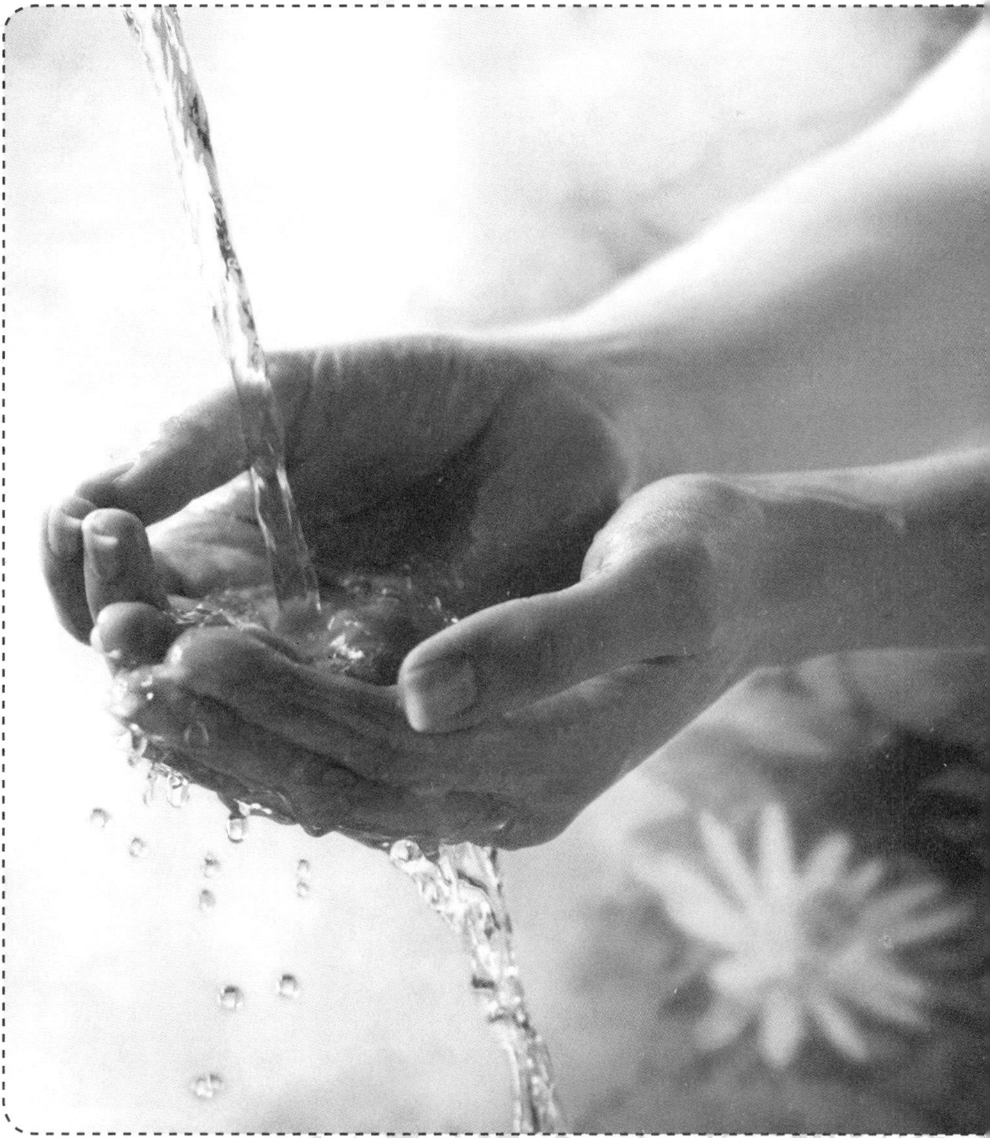

Scrub

- Who do you know who has rough hands?
- How can coming through rough situations help us in life?

Soothe

Read aloud:

The scrub has removed dead skin and left your skin a little vulnerable. You put on a soothing lotion and then dipped your hands in paraffin. The paraffin that is sealed around your hands is keeping in warmth and moisture. It is protecting your hands and soothing them.

- Which people offer protection and soothing for you when you're feeling vulnerable?

- How does Jesus protect and soothe you when you're in vulnerable situations?

- Psalm 139:5 affirms that God knows everything about us and is always with us. Verse 5b says, "You place your hand of blessing on my head." What does this verse mean to you?

Pray

After your discussion, remove the wax from your hands and dispose of the used wax and plastic bag.

The woman wearing the most orange should put cream on her hands and massage her partner's hands. As you massage, pray for your partner. You can pray silently or aloud, depending on what you're most comfortable with. Pray for some of the things your partner shared with you.

Then switch so both of you have an opportunity to pray for the other while giving a hand massage.

HOW TO GIVE A PEDICURE

If you're giving a pedicure, follow these steps:

1. Visit with your partner while she soaks her feet for a few minutes. She will have questions for you to discuss together.

2. Take one of your partner's feet from the water, and pat it dry with her towel. Gently rub a generous amount of the peppermint foot mask on your partner's foot, including the top of her foot, between her toes, and up to her ankle. Set this foot on the edge of the towel while you use the other end of the towel to dry her other foot. Apply mask to this foot as well.

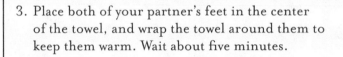

3. Place both of your partner's feet in the center of the towel, and wrap the towel around them to keep them warm. Wait about five minutes.

4. Unwrap your partner's feet, and let her put them back into the foot bath. Gently splash water over her feet and rub them in the water to remove the mask.

5. Dry your partner's feet, and gently massage them with peppermint lotion.

6. Empty the basin and refill it with warm water. Your Pampering Pedicures HeartSpa Station Leader will provide you with more peppermint foot soak. Switch places, and it's your turn for a pedicure!

DISCUSSION 1

As your partner is pampering your feet, read these questions aloud and the two of you can share your thoughts.

- Why are most people uncomfortable with touching feet or having others touch their feet?

- Tell about the funniest or most outrageous pair of shoes you've ever worn. Why did you choose them?

- Tell about your most comfortable shoes. What makes them so great?

IF YOU FINISH THIS DISCUSSION AND STILL HAVE TIME, ASK YOUR PARTNER A FEW QUESTIONS AND GET TO KNOW HER BETTER!

DISCUSSION 2

As your partner is pampering your feet, read these questions aloud and the two of you can share your thoughts.

- Think about the words you used to describe your comfortable shoes. Do any of these words describe your relationship with Jesus? If so, which ones?

PSALM 139:1-3 SAYS, "O LORD, YOU HAVE EXAMINED MY HEART AND KNOW EVERYTHING ABOUT ME. YOU KNOW WHEN I SIT DOWN OR STAND UP. YOU KNOW MY THOUGHTS EVEN WHEN I'M FAR AWAY. YOU SEE ME WHEN I TRAVEL AND WHEN I REST AT HOME. YOU KNOW EVERYTHING I DO."

- This passage affirms that Jesus knows all about us. How can this knowledge help you feel more comfortable in your relationship with Jesus?

A Closer Look

Read this during your personal quiet time or with your roommate during the HeartSpa Getaway.

Jesus Talks With the Samaritan Woman

Read John 4:4-30, 39-42. If you don't have your Bible handy, you can find the passage on page 6 of this HeartSpa Journal.

At the start of this Bible passage, we find Jesus stopping at a well to sit down and have a drink. It was in the heat of the day—a good time for a drink of water, but not the normal time for someone to come to draw water. The fact that the woman Jesus talked to was at the well around noon indicates that she was an outcast—someone not welcome at the well in the morning or evening when other women came. The woman must have known that Jesus realized her outcast status, and this added to her astonishment when he asked her for a drink. As a woman and a Samaritan, she would never have spoken to a Jew.

The division between Jews and Samaritans goes back to the time the Jews returned from captivity in Babylon. The Samaritans were the descendants of Jews who stayed in Palestine and intermarried with people of other groups living in the area. Such marriages were forbidden in Hebrew law, and thus the Jews chose to have no association with Samaritans. Jesus would have been made ceremonially unclean by drinking from a container that had been handled by a Samaritan.

Notice that we never read of Jesus getting a drink of water. It's possible that the woman gave him one, but her response to his initial request was apparently a refusal. Jesus was more concerned about the woman's relationship with God than about his own thirst. He knew that the woman needed the *living* water he could offer more than he needed to quench his physical thirst.

Also notice that we never read of the woman taking any water from the well. She leaves her jar when she goes back to the village. This serves as another reminder that she was filled with living water, and her physical needs for water were diminished at that point.

When Jesus spoke to the woman about living water, she didn't laugh at him and walk away, as one might have expected her to do. Although she didn't understand exactly what he was talking about, she continued the dialogue and questioned him further. Bit by bit Jesus got through to her, and eventually she understood.

The Samaritan woman made a point to tell everyone she knew about Jesus. She found "living water," and she wanted all her loved ones to "taste" what a friendship with Jesus was like. With whom are you sharing living water?

> **the 1 thing** *The 1 Thing: Your connection with Jesus is your living water. As you cultivate your friendship with Jesus through prayer and time in the Bible, you'll discover refreshment—even during parched times.*

The following devotions are provided for you to use after the HeartSpa Getaway. Use them and the blank pages that follow to "keep your sponge soaked" and spend time deepening your relationship with Jesus.

An Invitation You Can't Refuse

"WHEN JESUS CAME BY, HE LOOKED UP AT ZACCHAEUS AND CALLED HIM BY NAME. 'ZACCHAEUS!' HE SAID. 'QUICK, COME DOWN! I MUST BE A GUEST IN YOUR HOME TODAY'" (LUKE 19:5).

Have you ever been in a large crowd straining to see someone famous? What if that person suddenly turned to you and invited himself or herself to your house? What an honor—but *yikes!* The dishes aren't done, the laundry is on the sofa, and the cupboard is bare!

Has anyone ever "dropped by" when you felt your house was in total chaos? Did you find yourself more concerned with the appearance of your home than with your friendship? Most of our friends would follow common etiquette and call us before they showed up at our doorstep. But we have one friend who loves to "drop by" unexpectedly: Jesus!

When Zacchaeus climbed the tree, he never imagined he would be running home to make dinner for Jesus! And remember Peter and Matthew? They were busy working when Jesus suddenly showed up and said, "Follow me." There was no time for cleaning the house, checking the schedule, or coordinating a turnover of the business. A tree was jumped out of, nets were put down, and tax money was left on the table. It was an invitation they just couldn't refuse!

What if Jesus "dropped by" and invited himself into your life today? Would you say, "You'll have to wait until I get my house cleaned up" or "Let me check my schedule first"?

Finding time to spend with Jesus in the midst of our busy lives can be a real challenge—for us. For Jesus, anytime is a good time. Why? He's our only friend who is *always* with us, 24 hours a day, seven days a week. Even when the house is a mess, our hair is a mess, and our emotions are a mess, Jesus wants to be with us.

Shouldn't we have our times of devotion, prayer, and Bible reading properly scheduled and neatly organized? Wouldn't it please Jesus to see our lives neat and in order? Yes, those specifically prepared times *are* special to him, but...he wants more.

He wants us to search for him in the crowds of life. He wants us to feel his constant knocking on the door of our hearts. He wants us to hear our names being called over the buzz of our busyness. He's less concerned with our houses. What he really wants is our hearts—24/7.

Can you hear Jesus calling *your* name today? Can you forget how your house looks, drop everything, and spend some time with your best friend—the King?

Daily Challenge®

☐ Write out Luke 19:5-6 and insert your name in place of Zacchaeus'. Post your "invitation" from Jesus in a visible place, and respond to him as he "drops by" for a quick visit throughout your day!

• What "messes" in your life are you afraid Jesus will find if he drops in?

29

Sowing Tears, Reaping Joy!

"THOSE WHO PLANT IN TEARS WILL HARVEST WITH SHOUTS OF JOY. THEY WEEP AS THEY GO TO PLANT THEIR SEED, BUT THEY SING AS THEY RETURN WITH THE HARVEST" (PSALM 126:5-6).

Can you remember the first time you tried to pick a rose? *Owie!* Picking flowers wasn't supposed to hurt. You may not have realized it at the time, but you learned an important lesson that day: Life has thorns!

Jesus told us that here on earth we would "have many trials and sorrows" (John 16:33). Simply put, life hurts—and often more than a pricked finger. The pain of our trials and sorrows is usually unexpected, and sometimes these hurts become lasting wounds, slow to heal and difficult to treat.

We see these hurting women, these "walking wounded" all around us. You work with them. You're friends with them. You go to church with them. You may even *be* one of them...

Jesus warned us that life can hurt. Many of us will experience an extended trial or sorrow as a dark night of the soul. During this time of intense emotional pain, our faith may feel nearly extinguished. Despair may overtake our hope. We may even question God: "Will this dark night *ever* end?"

The good news is that in nature, *every* night ends with a morning. It's a promise we can count on. And likewise, for our dark nights of the soul, God promises us, "Weeping may last through the night, but joy comes with the morning" (Psalm 30:5).

Can we count on it? Dare we believe that God can transform our sorrows into joy? Yes!

Isaiah 25:8 says, "The Sovereign Lord will wipe away all tears," and Jeremiah 31:13 says, "I will comfort them and exchange their sorrow for rejoicing."

God's promises are so wonderful yet sometimes so unimaginable. In spite of what we feel, we can count on God to always to be the same. Just as morning dawns over a dark earth and spring follows winter, God promises us an "after" for our pain—healing for our hurting hearts and rejoicing for our sorrows!

All God requires of us is that we plant his seeds of promise in our hearts and water them with our tears. May we sow until our joy blooms once again!

Daily Challenge®

☐ *In a small pot, plant a flower seed that represents God's promise for healing your wounded heart. Decorate your pot with Scripture promises for hope and healing, perhaps choosing one mentioned above. As you water and nurture your seed, ask God to show you how he is nurturing* **you.** *Note the progress of your seed's growth and your healing on a page in this journal. Rejoice when you bloom together!*

• What are hurts or sorrows you've already seen turned to joy? What are ones you're still placing before God?

Prayer

Father, my gardener, I give you the tears of my hurting heart. May they water the seeds of your promises and yield a harvest of joy in the spring!

The Art of Prayer

"I AM PRAYING TO YOU BECAUSE I KNOW YOU WILL ANSWER, O GOD. BEND DOWN AND LISTEN AS I PRAY" (PSALM 17:6).

Good morning! Pour yourself a cup of coffee and pull up a chair so we can chat. In fact, why don't we begin with a word of prayer? "Our most gracious heavenly Father, who knowest what we needst and supplieth it…"

OK, now that we have had a word of prayer, why don't we have a word *about* prayer? Why does the thought of talking to God intimidate us so much? Is it because we think that we must sound so stiff and formal?

No doubt, prayer is important to God. Jesus prayed consistently and taught his followers to do the same. He wants to hear from us in the same way! Yet we fret too much over what to say and how to say it. If we speak, we want our words to sound like a work of art to God's ears. However, we get so busy agonizing over our would-be prayer life that we forget to actually pray. Today, let's freshen up our approach to conversation with God.

Think about your favorite friend. This friend knows the sound of your voice, your tone, the words you're likely to use, and the ones you never use. You know the same about your friend. You know each other inside and out.

Guess what? God knows *you* inside and out. His desire is for you to know him intimately as well. Jesus desires comfortable communication with you. So forget the fancy lingo. Forget how someone else might address the Almighty. The Lord wants you to talk to him the way *you* talk. Imagine yourself pulling up a chair and chatting with Jesus as your dearest friend. The more you chat, the dearer you become to each other.

You know, prayer has wonderful benefits. God will never be in the middle of a meal when you call. He abhors gossip, so your secrets are safe. He understands anger, confusion, and fear. You'll feel better after talking things out with him. You can tell him anything! He loves honesty. He lives to forgive. Just remember one thing as you pray: God is leaning close to hear from you. To him, your words are a masterpiece.

Daily Challenge®

Spend time today talking to Jesus. Simply start by telling God what you like about him, thanking him for what he does, and telling him about your needs.

. *What's on your mind right now that you'd like to share with God? Remember, just be yourself!*

Prayer

Jesus, today I commit to spending more time with you so we can become the very best of friends.

"GIVE YOUR GIFTS IN PRIVATE, AND YOUR FATHER, WHO SEES
EVERYTHING, WILL REWARD YOU" (MATTHEW 6:4).

"Hershey's Kisses! My favorite!" Sue exclaimed as she found the
surprise gift on her desk. Somebody knew it was her favorite treat.
But who?

Have you ever been the recipient of a secret gift? Maybe you
participated in a secret-Santa exchange at your work or a secret-pal
gift exchange with a group of your friends. Remember the thrill of
discovering that unexpected special treat? Did you have fun as the
secret giver, shopping and scheming to keep your identity a secret?

While you were covertly giving and receiving gifts, did you ever
realize that you were doing exactly what God calls *all* of us to do? To
God, giving in secret is more than just fun—it's the Christian way!

God calls us to be cheerful and secretive givers, but sometimes we
just don't know how or what to give. In Acts 3:6, Peter told a lame
man, "I don't have any silver or gold for you. But I'll give you what I
have." Have you ever felt like you were broke and had nothing to give?
Like Peter, we are never broke—as Christians we always have *something* to
give, and that something is *Jesus!*

Yet Jesus told us to give our gifts in secret. Why? Because a
wonderful thing happens when we give in secret. Instead of the gift
being given by us, it is given directly from the heart of Jesus! That's why
secret gifts are so special to receive and so fun to give. They're a secret
service for God!

Think of the fun you could have if you joined with friends and
started a "secret service squad" for God. You could keep a stash of
Hershey's Hugs to sneak onto that stressed-out co-worker's desk. You
could send anonymous notes of encouragement to your pastor and
ministry workers. Make cookies for the youth group, send pizza to
the nurses at the hospital, leave a teddy bear for a friend who needs
comfort—the ideas are endless!

So is Jesus' love! Join his "secret service squad" and put his love
into action!

Daily Challenge®

☐ *Give at least one secret love gift today. Even a note with a word of
encouragement can be a secret gift of your heart and time. Be sneaky
and have fun!*

What is an ability God's given you that you could share with others?

Prayer

Lord, may I be a blessing as I reach out to others and bless them with the gift of your love. May I freely give of the love I have freely received from you.

Oh, How Firm a Foundation!

"I WILL SHOW YOU WHAT IT'S LIKE WHEN SOMEONE COMES TO ME, LISTENS TO MY TEACHING, AND THEN FOLLOWS IT. IT IS LIKE A PERSON BUILDING A HOUSE WHO DIGS DEEP AND LAYS THE FOUNDATION ON SOLID ROCK" (LUKE 6:47-48a).

Barbara felt like it was the end of the world for her. As a younger woman, she had never imagined she'd be divorced and raising a child on her own. Yet here she was in that very situation. To make matters worse, her family was far away and her income was small. The world seemed hopeless.

She anguished, "But I'm a Christian now! Why is this happening to me?"

Barbara had to decide if her faith was going to be big. Despite being on shaky ground, she had to decide if God was indeed God. It took awhile before trust resurfaced. Healing did not happen overnight. Yet because of her faith, her foundation held firm.

As women, we can relate to the feelings of helplessness Barbara felt. Our circumstances may wear different labels, but we've all experienced the earthquakes that threaten our reality and even our sanity. These times may temporarily shake us up, but with Christ as our unshakable foundation, we won't be moved.

Think about this. Builders do tremendous research and testing on the ground when they build. They must ensure that their foundation will withstand the ravages of time. Why? Because they know what nature can dish out.

Contrast this firm and well-planned foundation with a sandy beach. Sure, the sand is pretty, but it can slow you down. And when the wind blows or the surf pounds, the sand shifts or blows away.

At any time, our circumstances can howl, and difficulties can wash over us like a tidal wave. Without the security of a firm foundation in Christ, we risk devastating consequences.

How firm is your foundation? Who or what is your solid rock? Society portrays security as money, power, jobs, marriage, health, and family. This security is fleeting and can vanish with a broken relationship, a phone call from the doctor, or an ill-timed merger. What happens then? Do we fall off the edge or do we stand on our feet?

Trusting in Jesus provides more security than people or money do. It doesn't mean we will never face adversity. However, it does ensure that when the storms of life rock our world, the Rock will not let us crumble. We may wobble and we may hit our knees (a preferable place to be), but our Anchor will hold.

Daily Challenge®

☐ Make a list of your current trials. Next to this, make a list of all the past times God has provided unmovable assistance. Be specific. Use this list to let the fulfillment of God's past promises help you now. Perhaps you and a struggling friend could do this together. Encourage each other to stand firm with Jesus!

What am I clinging to that makes my foundation feel shaky?

Prayer

Lord, I choose this day to live upon the foundation of your love, grace, mercy, and unmovable strength. Keep me walking steadily, hand in hand with you.

37

Sticks and Stones

"DON'T REPAY EVIL FOR EVIL. DON'T RETALIATE WITH INSULTS WHEN PEOPLE INSULT YOU. INSTEAD, PAY THEM BACK WITH A BLESSING. THAT IS WHAT GOD HAS CALLED YOU TO DO, AND HE WILL BLESS YOU FOR IT" (1 PETER 3:9).

Most of our mothers taught us, "Sticks and stones may break my bones, but words will never hurt me." Sadly, words often hurt more deeply and for a longer time than a broken bone. And even worse, Christians aren't immune from using words to hurt others.

Ask Chris, a young girl experiencing the flurry of insanity we call "the teenage years." She was new at church but met a kindred spirit right away. While parents are paramount in their kids' lives, there is something about a shoulder the same age and size as yours. Thus, Chris and her friend shared the good, the bad, and the ugly.

Alas, confessions made in confidence wound up on a teen hotline courtesy of her new friend. Concern for Chris was neatly disguised as a "prayer request." The result was more pain than Chris started out with. Those words hurt.

And then there's Gail. She bubbled and bounced all the way to Sunday service. She was excited because she was going to begin teaching seventh-grade Sunday school. Grand thoughts circled through her mind like horses on a merry-go-round. Even though she was a new Christian, she marveled at this new opportunity to share her faith.

Around the same time, the preschool director of the church also extended a teaching invitation to Gail. Although honored, Gail declined because of her prior commitment. The director's haughty response was, "Well, let's not get ahead of ourselves." That unkind comment haunted Gail and caused her doubt and concern about whether she was right to teach seventh grade after all. She started to second-guess herself and God. More words that hurt.

The Bible warns about guarding our speech. Ephesians 4:29 states, "Don't use foul or abusive language. Let everything you say be good and helpful, so that your words will be an encouragement to those who hear them." In Matthew 7, Jesus talks about not judging others lest we stand judged ourselves.

Let's let our relationships be shining examples of integrity and love. Let's be women who are known for building others up instead of tearing them down. Consider your intent before sharing "prayer requests." Consider the feelings and privacy of others before speaking of their situations. And remember, you can always talk to God about everything without breaking a confidence or gossiping.

Daily Challenge

☐ Ask God to bring to your mind one person who has been hurt by the words of another (perhaps even you). Then call or visit that person with two cups of kindness and a quart of encouragement. Throw in a smile just for fun. (And a cup of coffee never hurts either!) Then see who gets the most blessing.

What do the words I speak reflect about my heart and attitudes?

Prayer

Father God, guard my mouth so I don't speak against those you love so much. Let me make someone smile before the sun sets today.

Peace Treats With Jesus

"I AM LEAVING YOU WITH A GIFT—PEACE OF MIND AND HEART. AND THE PEACE I GIVE IS A GIFT THE WORLD CANNOT GIVE. SO DON'T BE TROUBLED OR AFRAID" (JOHN 14:27).

Take a moment to think about a recent experience you had where you felt the need for peace. Perhaps it was today in the slow checkout line at your local superstore or last week when you were stuck in traffic and late for an appointment.

In our busy lives, a moment of peace would be a special treat—like the little chocolate left on our pillow at a luxury hotel. Have you ever eaten that chocolate and felt guilty later? If you took the time for a "peace treat"—a moment of rest in your strenuous schedule—would you feel guilty about that, too?

When was the last time you enjoyed a "peace treat"? We women commonly experience more stress than peace in our lives. This is a real problem for us. Medical research estimates that as much as 90 percent of our illnesses and diseases are stress-related. And, as women, we are nearly twice as likely as men to be afflicted with them.

Stress is making us sick! We need a prescription for a rejuvenating Hawaiian vacation or spa retreat! These breaks aren't just a luxury item anymore. We need peace as a daily requirement for health!

Let's get practical. We need to get an everyday dose of "peace treats," such as a hot cup of tea, a nap, or a good book. Unfortunately, without Jesus even these will be incomplete.

The good news is that Jesus has given us a *free gift* of peace, and it's available anytime and anywhere! The Bible says that this peace is different from the peace the world can give us. The world can give us rest, but God gives us *peace of mind and heart!*

We need more peace—both as the world gives *and* as Jesus gives. We need to give ourselves those "peace treats" of the restful activities we enjoy, *and* we need to ask for the wonderful "gift of peace" that only Jesus can give.

How do you receive his peace? Add some Scripture meditation or prayer to your tea time. Ask Jesus for peace of mind the next time you're in the slow checkout line or "stressing out" over life. He's got peace, and he can give it!

Indulge yourself, enjoy some "peace treats" with Jesus, and forget the guilt!

Daily Challenge®

☐ *Make a list of your favorite relaxing activities and your favorite Bible verses about peace. Place the lists in a special gift box. Choose an activity and a Scripture each day to enjoy a special "peace treat" time with Jesus.*

What makes it hard for you to enjoy times of peace?

_____

_____

_____

_____

_____

_____

_____

_____

_____

_____

_____

_____

_____

_____

_____

_____

_____

_____

Prayer

God of all peace, fill my mind and heart today with the gift of peace that only you can give!

41

Cinderella Seasons

"YOU MUST HAVE THE SAME ATTITUDE THAT CHRIST JESUS HAD" (PHILIPPIANS 2:5).

Wouldn't we all like to be Cinderella? At least the part of the story from Prince Charming to happily ever after. Alas, from time to time, most of us feel like we're stuck in a never-ending episode of "Cinderella: The Early Years."

We wash, cook, clean, and then clean some more, along with answering phone calls only to discover the latest sales pitch and cramming in those 40 hours for the boss. And let's not forget about those with husbands—that's a whole other story. Cinderella may not be the only one talking to mice!

Where are the seasons of refreshment we yearn for? Where is the peace and fulfillment in life? Where is Prince Charming and happily ever after?

One step to finding them is to start with a little thing called *attitude*. Nine times out of 10, circumstances are only exasperating when we look at them with an attitude of frustration. When the attitude changes, those same situations often look different.

God gives each of us tasks, some mundane and some mighty. When we wash clothes for our family, we can do it with a grudge or we can do it as if we're serving Jesus. When we deliver a meal, we can slam it on the table or place it as a gift to God. When we take time with a child or friend in need, we can be grouches or filled with joy.

It's all in the attitude. While life is full of Cinderella seasons, it seldom overflows with long gowns, tiaras, and palaces where you never have to dust. Life overflows with life, day by day, moment by moment, and heart by heart. And when we ask God to give us attitudes like his own, the princess that hides underneath the ashes and dirt emerges.

Jesus, being God, put aside his glory and gave his life for us. He served without regard to time, energy, or cost. And he did it gladly. To touch hearts in the name of Jesus—now that's a *real* Cinderella season.

Daily Challenge

☐ Examine an area of your life that you're not viewing with a Christ-like attitude. Write it down. Ask God to adjust your attitude and guide you in a specific action to take. Then do it (with a smile!).

• Where do you need the biggest attitude adjustment? What could happen if you change your perspective?

_____
_____
_____
_____
_____
_____
_____
_____
_____
_____
_____
_____
_____
_____
_____

Prayer

Precious Jesus, I desire more than anything to have the same attitude as you. Please create in me a Christ-centered heart, mind, and attitude.

"SINCE GOD CHOSE YOU TO BE THE HOLY PEOPLE HE LOVES, YOU MUST CLOTHE YOURSELVES WITH TENDERHEARTED MERCY, KINDNESS, HUMILITY, GENTLENESS, AND PATIENCE" (COLOSSIANS 3:12).

It's the first thought women have upon entering their closets. It strikes fear into the hearts of anyone within shrieking range. *"I don't have a thing to wear!"*

OK, so most of us have plenty of clothing. We just don't want to be caught wearing any of it. And regardless of what the media tell us, nakedness is generally frowned upon. Therefore, with great pains, we dress before leaving the house, trying to avoid any fashion faux pas. We go to great lengths to appropriately wear each article of clothing, yet we often miswear our emotions.

That's right, our emotions—forces more powerful than a crazed shopaholic. Often, they rush up on us before we can even get them off the hanger! True, the emotions we have are from God. They make up our emotional closet—emotions like anger, jealousy, compassion, mercy, and love. Each is present in us and a permanent part of us.

However, just as we stand in front of our clothes to pick the right attire for the occasion, we should choose the right emotions as well. Then we must wear them properly. Wearing clothes inside out, backward, or twisted (like the infamous pantyhose) is uncomfortable and often embarrassing. Emotions displayed improperly have the same results. You see, there is a proper way to wear emotions, even the ones we consider negative.

It would help us to remember Colossians 3:14. It advises, "Above all, clothe yourselves with love, which binds us all together in perfect harmony." Love is our spiritual suspenders, holding everything up and lessening the risk of us getting caught with our pants down.

We have a model for our emotional behavior in Jesus Christ. Whether defending children, tossing out money-changers, or answering endless questions from the disciples, he did so honestly and justly. If we use the Lord as our standard, we will consistently find ourselves not dressed to kill but righteously dressed for any occasion.

Daily Challenge®

☐ *Make a list of the emotions you remember feeling so far today. Circle the ones that you need to work on wearing less often or that you need to wear more appropriately. Then list any additions you'd like to make to your emotional closet. Use this as a prayer list; then put it into action.*

· Consider yourself "dressed" in emotions. Which ones make you feel most beautiful?

"THE LORD IS MY SHEPHERD; I SHALL NOT WANT" (PSALM 23:1, KING JAMES VERSION).

Can you imagine telling 2-year-olds that they "shall not want"? They *do* want! They want candy bars at the store. They want their siblings' toys. They want doughnuts for dinner. A child wants a lot of things, but a parent can say "no" if it's something the child doesn't *need.*

As grown women, we have "wants," too. And sometimes our wants are not so different (bring on the chocolate!). But we have a heavenly Father who can say "no." Just like a 2-year-old, we don't always get what we *want,* but 2 Peter 1:3 says, "By his divine power, God has given us everything we need for living a godly life."

When life gets stressful, we may think we really *need* that chocolate bar! But the Lord knows what we *really* need. He's aware of the stresses and messes of our lives, and he knows when we're hungry, tired, or afraid. He hears our cries for help. He carries us when we are too weak to go on. He searches for us when we become hopelessly lost.

God shepherds us with love because we are "the sheep of his pasture" (Psalm 100:3). He knows that our deepest wants *are* our needs. Life is exhausting—we need rest. Life is chaotic—we need peace. Life is lonely—we need love. Life is difficult—we need help! God answers our wants by promising us exactly what we need.

The Lord is our shepherd. We shall not want. Read the translation of Psalm 23 on page 48. Then consider, what is your deepest "want" today?

Daily Challenge®

☐ *On the next page, make your own "want" list with matching Scripture promises. Keep it handy. Whenever you have a "want," refer to God's answer for just what you **need**!*

• What are your wants and needs? How do these compare to God's promises for your life?

_____
_____
_____
_____
_____
_____
_____
_____
_____
_____
_____
_____
_____
_____
_____

Prayer

Heavenly Father, my Lord and shepherd, hear the "wants" of my heart today and give me everything I need!

I want someone to help me.	"The Lord is my shepherd; I have all that I need.
I want rest.	He lets me rest in green meadows;
I want peace.	He leads me beside peaceful streams.
I want strength.	He renews my strength.
I want guidance.	He guides me along right paths, bringing honor to his name.
I want courage.	Even when I walk through the darkest valley, I will not be afraid, for you are close beside me.
I want to feel safe.	Your rod and your staff protect and comfort me.
I want to overcome adversity.	You prepare a feast for me in the presence of my enemies.
I want to feel valued.	You honor me by anointing my head with oil.
I want to feel blessed.	My cup overflows with blessings.
I want to be loved.	Surely your goodness and unfailing love will pursue me all the days of my life,
I want a home.	and I will live in the house of the Lord forever."

You've experienced HeartSpa™—
now share it with your friends and neighbors

HeartSpa Retreat Kit

Now that you've experienced HeartSpa, plan your own getaway with your friends, sisters, daughters, youth group, for a birthday party, or at your small group.

HeartSpa Kit includes:

- **Director's Guide**
  (includes a CD-ROM packed with reproducible materials!)

- **Worship Leader's Guide**
  (includes a CD-ROM with full vocal version and instrumental-only version of each song, plus PowerPoint slides!)

- **Leader Guides:**
  * Lessons for the Heart: Session 1
  * Lessons for the Heart: Session 2
  * Lessons for the Heart: Session 3
  * Healing Hands HeartSpa Station
  * Pampering Pedicures HeartSpa Station
  * Refreshing Facials HeartSpa Station
  * Heart-to-Home Creations:
    Sugar & Spice Spa Set
  * Heart-to-Home Creations: Comfort Pillow

- **HeartSpa Journal**

- **Training and Promotion DVD**

- **Sample Crafts:**
  * 1 Sugar & Spice Spa Set
  * 1 Comfort Pillow

- **Sample Pack**
  * Name Tag
  * 11 x 17 Promo Poster
  * 11 x 17 Getaway Shop Poster
  * Invitation Postcard Sheet
  * Follow-up Postcard Sheet
  * Full Sticker Sheet
  * Gift Tag

You get all this for only **$99.99**

tasting is believing

ve HeartSpa?
Sink your teeth into...

Group's
CHOCOLATE BOUTIQUE
Where Women Taste and See That the Lord Is Good